Bond Assessment Papers

Third papers in English

J M Bond and Sarah Lindsay

Key words

Some special words are used in this book. You will find them picked out in **bold** in the Papers. These words are explained here.

abbreviation	a word or words which are shortened
acronym	a word or letter string made up from the initial letters of other words
adjective	a word that describes somebody or something
adverb	a word that gives extra meaning to a verb
alphabetical order	words arranged in the order found in the alphabet
antonym	a word with a meaning opposite to another word *hot – cold*
clause	a section of a sentence with a verb
compound word	a word made up of two other words *football*
conjunction	a word used to link sentences, phrases or words *and, but*
connective	a word or words that join clauses or sentences
contraction	two words shortened into one with an apostrophe placed where the letter/s have been dropped *do not = don't*
definition	meanings of words
dialect	regional variations of vocabulary in the spoken language
diminutive	a word implying smallness *booklet*
future tense	something that will or may happen
homophone	words that have the same sound as another but a different meaning or spelling *right / write*
noun	a word for somebody or something
collective noun	a word referring to a group *swarm*
proper noun	the names of people, places etc. *Ben*
abstract noun	a word referring to a concept or idea *love*
onomatopoeic	a word that echoes a sound, associated with its meaning *hiss*
past tense	something that has already happened
phrase	a group of words that act as a unit
adjectival phrase	a group of words describing a noun
plural	more than one *cats*
prefix	a group of letters added to the beginning of a word *un, dis*
preposition	a word that relates other words to each other – *he sat <u>behind</u> me, the book <u>on</u> the table*
present tense	something happening now
pronoun	words often replacing nouns
personal pronoun	pronouns used when writing about ourselves *I, you*
possessive pronoun	a pronoun showing to whom something belongs *mine, ours, his, hers, yours, theirs*
reported speech	what has been said without using the exact words or speech marks
root word	words to which prefixes or suffixes can be added to make other words <u>*quick*</u>*ly*
singular	one *cat*
suffix	a group of letters added to the end of a word *ly, ful*
synonym	words with a very similar meaning to another word *quick – fast*
verb	a 'doing' or 'being' word

Paper 1

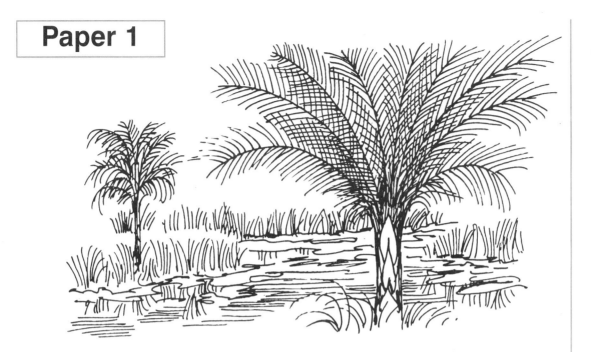

Raffia

Raffia is a kind of palm tree that grows on the islands around Madagascar. The leaves of this tree grow to nearly fifteen metres in length. The material we know as raffia comes from these leaves. The inner skins of the leaves are peeled and then stretched out in the tropical sun, which dries and bleaches them. The dried raffia is made up into hanks, and sold by weight. Natural raffia is a creamy colour but it can be dyed very easily. If you find the raffia stiff to handle you can soak it for an hour or two in water, and leave it to dry. Raffia can be plaited, twisted, woven, knotted, stitched and embroidered.

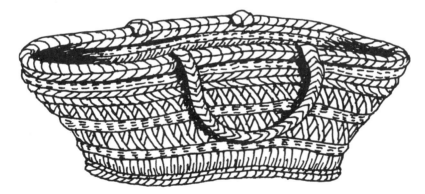

Underline the correct answers.

1 Raffia is a kind of (grass, rush, palm tree).

2 (The inside, The outside, The peel) of the leaf is used to make the raffia that we know.

3 Raffia leaves can be softened by (peeling them, bleaching them, wetting them).

Answer these questions.

4 Where do raffia trees grow?

_____

5 Approximately how long are the leaves of the raffia tree?

_____

6–7 Why are the inner skins of the leaves that make raffia stretched out in the sun?

_____

8 Why do you think raffia is sold by weight?

_____

9–10 Name two things that can be made from raffia.

_____   _____

7

Underline the correct **homophone** in each bracket.

11–12 The (scent, sent) of the flowers you (scent, sent) me is strong.

13–14 Tom (threw, through) the ball (threw, through) the window.

15–16 The (not, knot) joining these ropes is (not, knot) tied tightly.

17–18 Michelle cut her hand on the (pain, pane) of glass and the (pain, pane) is very bad.

19–20 I saw him (stair, stare) at the man on the (stairs, stares).

10

Put these words in **alphabetical order**.

flame   fire   flood   first   flap   flop

21 (1) _____   **22** (2) _____

23 (3) _____   **24** (4) _____

25 (5) _____   **26** (6) _____

6

Add the missing commas to these sentences.

27–29 Sam loved going for walks swimming in the duck pond chasing rabbits chewing a bone and sleeping in front of the fire.

30–31 The baby cries when it is tired hungry has a tummy ache or has a dirty nappy.

32–34 Jack wanted a new bike some colouring pens a computer game new trainers and a pet dog for his birthday!

8

Circle the **nouns**.

35–41   gatepost   fetched   York   Monday

        bunch   banana   under   frighten

        fought   violin   team   sunny

7

Choose an **adverb** to fill each gap.

         suddenly   neatly   heavily   soundly

              smartly   greedily   swiftly

42   Kim _____ wrote a letter.

43   The old tramp _____ ate his food.

44   All day the rain fell _____ .

45   The child slept _____ .

46   The boy ran _____ in the race.

47   The car braked _____ .

48   The young lady always dressed _____ .

7

Write the **plural** form of each of these nouns.

49   telephone _____   **50**   lantern _____

51   museum _____   **52**   gorilla _____

53   chocolate _____   **54**   tissue _____

6

Add the missing punctuation at the end of each sentence.

55   Watch out, James is coming _____

56   Many people had left their homes _____

57   It must be time to have dinner _____

58   Where has your Grandad gone _____

59   Why do I have to brush my teeth every day _____

60   The snow dropped silently, covering the ground _____

61   Quick, the film is about to start _____

7

Rewrite these sentences changing them from **plural** to **singular**.

62–64 The girls ran to catch their buses.

_____

65–66 They had collected money to give to the homeless children.

_____

67–69 The lambs bounced towards their mothers.

_____

8

Underline the **pronouns** in the following passage.

70–75 We are going to Hull to see the docks. We will see several ships and if we are lucky they might let us look round them.

6

Underline one word in each group which is *not* a **synonym** for the rest.

76 hold   maintain   keep   destroy   retain

77 beautiful   nasty   lovely   pretty   handsome

78 happy   unwell   sick   ill   unhealthy

79 write   draw   scribble   sketch   kick

80 unhappy   sad   gloomy   upset   delighted

81 gigantic   enormous   big   tiny   large

6

Give Yourself a Hug

Give yourself a hug
when you feel unloved

Give yourself a hug
when people put on airs
to make you feel a bug

Give yourself a hug
when everyone seems to give you
a cold-shoulder shrug

Give yourself a hug –
a big big hug

And keep on singing
'Only one in a million like me
Only one in a million-billion-trillion-zillion
like me.'

by Grace Nichols

Answer these questions.

82 Which line in the poem repeats itself four times?

_____

83–84 Write two reasons listed in the poem, why you should 'give yourself a hug'.

_____

_____

85 What do you think 'a cold-shoulder shrug' means?

_____

86 Do you think the poet thinks that giving yourself a hug will make you feel better?

_____

87 What message do you think the final verse is giving to the reader?

_____

Write each of these words as an **adjective** by adding the **suffix** _ful_.

88 care _____

89 thought _____

90 hope _____

91 shame _____

92 wonder _____

93 deceit _____

Add the missing apostrophe for **plural nouns** to each of these **phrases**.

94 the three dogs collars

95 the two cars horns

96 the five girls jumpers

97 the two cinemas screens

98 the three boys books

99 the six birds beaks

100 the two houses chimneys

Paper 2

A Week of Winter Weather

On Monday icy rain poured down
and flooded drains all over town.
Tuesday's gales bashed elm and ash;
dead branches came down with a crash.
On Wednesday bursts of hail and sleet,
no-one walked along the street.
Thursday stood out clear and calm
but the sun was paler than my arm.
Friday's frost that bit your ears
was cold enough to freeze your tears.
Saturday's sky was ghostly grey;
we smashed ice on the lake today.
Christmas Eve was Sunday . . . and
snow fell and fell across the land.

by Wes Magee

Underline the correct answers.

1 On which day was there flooding?
(Monday, Wednesday, Friday)

2 On which day were we told there was no wind?
(Wednesday, Thursday, Saturday)

3 Which day of the week was Christmas Day?
(Sunday, Monday, Tuesday)

Answer these questions.

4–5 Name the two types of tree mentioned in the poem.

_____   _____

6–7 Which two days were frosty?

_____   _____

3

8–9 Write a word in the poem that rhymes with . . .

calm _____   and _____

10 Which is your favourite day of the week? Why?

_____

Find seven different **verbs** in the poem 'A Week of Winter Weather' by Wes Magee.

11–17

_____   _____   _____

_____   _____   _____

_____

Underline one **clause** (a section of a sentence with a verb) in each of these sentences.

18 The goats pushed their way out of their pen because they had spotted some apples.

19 The cars raced past us while we waited at the side of the motorway.

20 Matthew's present was quickly hidden under the sofa as he came in through the door.

21 Some children wanted to go swimming even though the water was freezing.

22 The hat fitted perfectly but it was the wrong colour.

23 It started to rain heavily as darkness fell over the sleepy village.

Underline the **root word** for each of these words.

24 unhappy   **25** jumped   **26** quickly

27 displacement   **28** uncertain   **29** affix

30 untie   **31** stronger   **32** mistrusted

Match a word with the same letter string but a different pronunciation, to each of these words.

height   foot   have   cough

drought   both   move   flower

33 bough _____   **34** weight _____

35 boot _____   **36** cave _____

9

37 moth _____	**38** love _____	
39 slower _____	**40** thought _____	**8**

Copy these sentences and write a **possessive pronoun** in place of the words in bold.

41–42 **Your hair** looks longer than **my hair**.

_____

43–44 **Our house** is smaller than **David's house**.

_____

45–46 **Their dog** runs faster than **our dog**.

_____

6

Write the masculine of each of the following words.

47 waitress _____	**48** aunt _____	
49 queen _____	**50** niece _____	
51 woman _____	**52** cow _____	
53 mother _____	**54** sister _____	**8**

Add the missing *ie* or *ei* letters to complete each word correctly.

55 ch_____f	**56** f_____ld	**57** w_____ght
58 bel_____ve	**59** _____ght	**60** rec_____ve
61 v_____n	**62** th_____r	**8**

Copy the **proper nouns**, adding the missing capital letters.

63–69
duck	prince edward	wednesday
ship	london	football
everton football club	lucy smith	cargo
river severn	gate	parklands primary school

_____   _____

_____   _____

_____   _____

_____

7

Add a **verb** to these sentences.

Run   Watch   Pass   Stop   Find   Hurry

70 _____ me a drink!

71 _____ out, you're standing on my toe!

72 _____ yourself a chair and sit down.

73 _____, he is going to catch you!

74 _____, a car is coming!

75 _____ up, we will be late!

6

Write two **antonyms** for each of these words.

76–77 big _____ _____

78–79 rough _____ _____

80–81 small _____ _____

6

Monday 6th October

©BBC

3.25	**Tweenies**	Bella, Milo, Fizz and Jake find out about cross-Channel ferries
3.45	**Bob the Builder**	Bob goes looking for a missing digger
3.55	**Rugrats**	Cartoon fun
4.20	**The Animal Magic Show**	Animals that jump
4.35	**SMart**	How to make models from rubbish and tips on drawing people
5.00	**Newsround**	All the day's current issues
5.10	**Blue Peter**	The launch of the new appeal and how to make mini fruit cakes

Answer these questions.

82 What are Bella, Milo, Fizz and Jake going to find out about?

_____

83 What would you be watching at 4.25?

_____

84 At what time would you watch a cartoon?

_____

85 Which programme gives you tips on drawing people?

_____

86 If you could only watch one programme, which would it be? Why?

_____

87 Which of these programmes do you think are more relevant to children of your age?

_____

6

Add different **adverbs** to each sentence.

88–89 The children sat in their seats _____ and continued with their work

_____ .

90–91 The children sat in their seats _____ and continued with their work

_____ .

92–93 The children sat in their seats _____ and continued with their work

_____ .

94–95 The children sat in their seats _____ and continued with their work

_____ .

8

Write a word to match each clue.

96 Long pieces of pasta   s_____

97 An animal from Australia that jumps   k_____

98 A hot drink, often drunk at breakfast   c_____

99 A red fruit, often served in salad   t_____

100 What do you notice about the last letter of each of the words above (Q. **96–99**)?

_____

5

100
TOTAL

Paper 3

I dared not stir out of my castle for days, lest some savage should capture me. However, I gained a little courage and went with much dread to make sure that the footprint was not my own. I measured my foot against it. Mine was not nearly so large. A stranger, maybe a savage, must have been on shore, and fear again filled my heart.

I determined now to make my house more secure than ever. I built another wall around it, in which I fixed six guns, so that, if need be, I could fire off six in two minutes. Then I planted young trees around. I feared my goats might be hurt or stolen from me, so I fenced round several plots of ground, as much out of sight as possible, and put some goats in each plot. All this while I lived with a terrible fear in my mind that I might one day meet an enemy. I had lived on this lonely island for eighteen years.

Once, when on the opposite side of the island, I was filled with horror; for on the ground I saw the remains of a fire, and also a number of human bones. This told me plainly that cannibals had been there.

From *Robinson Crusoe* by Daniel Defoe

Underline the correct answers.

1 How did Robinson Crusoe know the footprint was not his?
(It was a strange shape, It was larger than his, It was smaller than his)

2 How quickly could Robinson Crusoe fire his six guns?
(in 30 seconds, in one minute, in two minutes)

3 How long had Robinson Crusoe lived on the island?
(eighteen months, eight years, eighteen years)

3

Answer these questions.

4–5 Write two things Robinson Crusoe did to protect his house.

_____

_____

6 What did Robinson Crusoe fear might be hurt or stolen from him?

_____

7 What was Robinson Crusoe's greatest fear?

_____

8 Why did Robinson Crusoe think cannibals had been on the island?

_____

9-10 Write two words describing how you would feel if you suddenly discovered cannibals were living on the same island as you.

_____   _____

7

Underline the **nouns** in this passage.

11-21 My aunt, uncle and cousin came to stay with us last Wednesday. Next week we will catch a train to Birmingham. We are taking them to the theatre to see a pantomime called Aladdin. We will get back to our house very late.

11

Rewrite these sentences, adding the missing speech marks and other punctuation.

22-25 Come and hear the man play his banjo called Tim

_____

26-29 Where's my other slipper grumbled Grandpa

_____

8

Extend each of these words into a **compound word**.

30 tea_____   **31** sun_____

32 snow_____   **33** grand_____

34 pillow_____   **35** foot_____

36 tooth_____   **37** play_____

8

Write each of these words in its plural form.

38 brush _____   **39** church _____

40 punch _____   **41** bus _____

42 thrush _____   **43** dress _____

6

Underline the **reported speech** sentences (what has been said without using the exact words or speech marks).

44–47

"Time to go Sam," called Mum.
Hank shouted to Ben to hurry up.
Kay moaned that Debbie was always late.
"Tuhil, are you coming?" shouted his teacher.
"Let's take the dog for a walk," pleaded the children.
The teacher told the children to leave by the fire exit.
"We had sausages for tea," said Maeve.
Mum told Gran that David's school report was good.

4

Rewrite these words adding the **suffix** *ing* to each one.

48 drive _____   49 believe _____

50 make _____   51 care _____

52 close _____   53 waste _____

54 wake _____   55 hope _____

8

There is a lake near our town and it is very popular with both adults and children. The Sailing Club is at the south end of the lake and at the opposite end is a boathouse where visitors can hire various craft – sailing boats, rowing boats and canoes. Towards the middle of the lake on one side there is a part which is roped off. This is used for swimming. Sometimes a sailing boat capsizes, and as the water is not very deep this can provide much merriment for the onlookers! There are many reasons why a boat may capsize. Usually it is caused by a violent gust of wind, but it may be due to overloading, a faulty boat, or simply lack of skill in handling the craft.

Write *true* or *false* next to each statement.

56 The lake is only popular with children. _____

57 The sailing club is at the north end of the lake. _____

58 At the boathouse visitors can hire canoes. _____

59 There is an area for swimming in the lake. _____

60 The water in the lake is very deep. _____

61 Overloading can cause boats to capsize. _____

62 It is always the sailors' fault when a boat capsizes. _____

7

Write which animal these **onomatopoeic** words remind you of.

63 Quack! _____   64 Baa! _____

65 Neigh! _____   66 Woof! _____

67 Miaow! _____   68 Hiss! _____

Add the missing commas to these sentences.

69 The wind swept over the barren landscape tossing leaves high into the air.

70 Although the speeding train came off its rails no one was hurt.

71 The lion crept up on its prey ready to pounce.

72 Fed up because the computer continually broke down they decided to buy a new one.

73 The sunbathers lay on the beach all afternoon unaware of how burnt they were becoming.

74 Jess was delighted to see her mum though she wished she had come to collect her earlier.

Circle the words which have a soft c.

75–82   city   copy   cereal   face   magic   fleece

clown   mice   lace   accident   cabbage

vacuum   cat   jack   ace   carrot

With a line match the words with the same spelling patterns.

83 sound   match

84 high   hollow

85 fair   found

86 bridge   sigh

87 follow   fridge

88 hatch   chair

Rewrite each sentence as if you were writing about yourself.

e.g. He enjoys running.   *I enjoy running.*

89 They fell over.   _____

90 She feels hot.   _____

91 He plays football. _____

92 They walk home slowly. _____

93 She enjoys swimming. _____

94 They made some cakes. _____

6

Write a more powerful **verb** for each of these verbs.

95 said _____ **96** take _____

97 walk _____ **98** jump _____

99 make _____ **100** fall _____

6

100 TOTAL

Paper 4

A Servant for a Day by Kate Redman
23rd March

We arrived at Bourton House just after 10 o'clock. We were all dressed in Victorian costume. I was wearing a plain brown dress with black shoes and stockings. My hair was in a bun. I had a shawl to keep me warm.

As soon as we arrived we were told off for being late. I thought it wasn't our fault but was too scared to say anything.

Then we were given our instructions. We weren't allowed to talk, had to walk everywhere quietly and if we were spoken to, always had to say "Yes ma'am" or "Yes sir".

We were shown into the dining room where we were taught to fold napkins. It was very hard and Helen got told off for making a mess of hers.

Then we went into the kitchens and were taught how to bake bread. We all took it in turns to help, it was great fun and the cook was really nice. She didn't mind if we talked and laughed.

Suddenly we heard a bell in the corridor. The bell told us we were wanted in the bedrooms so we hurried up the stairs as quietly as possible. Dan fell over! There we were told how to make the bed and sweep the floor. When we swept the floor we had to put tea leaves down; as we swept them up it helped to pick up the dirt.

At last it was time to go back to school. We were told we had been good servants and if we ever wanted a job we could have one at Bourton House!

It was a great trip but I didn't like not being able to talk.

Underline the correct answers.

1 What period costume was Kate wearing?
(Viking, Victorian, don't know)

2 Why did Kate wear a shawl?
(to look good, to hide her dress, to keep her warm)

3 Which room were they shown into first?
(the kitchen, the dining room, the bedroom)

4 Who got told off while folding a napkin?
(Helen, Kate, Dan)

Answer these questions.

5–6 Write two of the instructions the children were given.

_____

_____

7 Which work did Kate enjoy the most?

_____

8 Why do you think tea leaves helped to pick up the dirt?

_____

9 Which part of the trip would you have enjoyed the most? Why?

_____

Add the **prefix** pro or bi to each of these words.

10	_____found	11	_____cycle	12	_____lingual		
13	_____vision	14	_____longed	15	_____plane		
16	_____position	17	_____noun				

Underline the correct form of the **verb** to complete each sentence.

18 The children watch/watches the match.

19 A cat play/plays with a mouse.

20 Winds sweep/sweeps across the land.

21 William run/runs to catch the bus.

22 The women win/wins the lottery.

23 Six children swim/swims for charity.

24 A leaf drop/drops from a tree.　　　　　　　　　　　　　　7

Write one word for each **definition**.

25 Part of a plant that grows downwards and draws food from the soil　　＿＿＿＿＿

26 The time between dusk and dawn　　＿＿＿＿＿

27 A grown-up person　　＿＿＿＿＿

28 A member of the army　　＿＿＿＿＿

29 A small white flower with a yellow centre　　＿＿＿＿＿

30 A line of people, one behind another, waiting for their turn
to do something　　＿＿＿＿＿　　6

Write two different sentences each ending with a question mark.

31 ＿＿＿＿＿＿＿＿＿＿＿＿＿＿＿＿＿＿＿＿＿＿＿＿＿＿＿＿＿＿＿＿＿

32 ＿＿＿＿＿＿＿＿＿＿＿＿＿＿＿＿＿＿＿＿＿＿＿＿＿＿＿＿＿＿＿＿＿　　2

Write two different sentences each ending with a full-stop.

33 ＿＿＿＿＿＿＿＿＿＿＿＿＿＿＿＿＿＿＿＿＿＿＿＿＿＿＿＿＿＿＿＿＿

34 ＿＿＿＿＿＿＿＿＿＿＿＿＿＿＿＿＿＿＿＿＿＿＿＿＿＿＿＿＿＿＿＿＿　　2

Write two different sentences each ending with an exclamation mark.

35 ＿＿＿＿＿＿＿＿＿＿＿＿＿＿＿＿＿＿＿＿＿＿＿＿＿＿＿＿＿＿＿＿＿

36 ＿＿＿＿＿＿＿＿＿＿＿＿＿＿＿＿＿＿＿＿＿＿＿＿＿＿＿＿＿＿＿＿＿　　2

Squirrels are found in most countries. In Europe it is the red squirrel that is seen most, but in Britain the grey squirrel has been introduced from America. Flying squirrels do not really fly but glide from one tree to another. Ground squirrels may dig large numbers of burrows.

Underline the statements below which are *true*.

37–41 There are only grey squirrels in Britain.

Flying squirrels glide.

Grey squirrels first came from America.

Squirrels are found in Europe and elsewhere.

There are not many squirrels now.

A squirrel's home is called a tunnel.

Flying squirrels live in America only.

Ground squirrels can dig a large number of burrows.

The most common squirrel in Europe is the red squirrel.

5

Add a different **adjective** in each gap to complete the sentences.

42 All the children liked the _____ classroom.

43 The Browns had a _____ clock in the hall.

44 The _____ spoon was used for cake-making.

45 They made a _____ crown for the king.

46 The _____ lady presented the prizes.

47 They went up the _____ staircase.

48 The _____ book looked as though it had been read many times.

49 The _____ kitten romped around the house.

8

Write the word for the young of each of these animals, e.g. sheep *lamb*.

50 dog _____   51 pig _____

52 cat _____   53 horse _____

54 cow _____   55 goat _____

56 duck _____   57 chicken _____

8

Rewrite these sentences without the double negatives.

58 I'm not never coming back.

_____

59 Mark hasn't brought no towel for swimming.

_____

60 The shopkeeper didn't have no fireworks.

_____

61 There wasn't no teacher to help with my spelling.

_____

62 Amy hasn't no coat to wear.

_____

63 There weren't no goats on the farm.

_____

| 6 |

Add the **suffix** to each word, first doubling a letter if you need to.

64 sit + ing _____   **65** stop + ed _____

66 get + ing _____   **67** walk + ed _____

68 grin + ing _____   **69** rot + ed _____

70 shop + ing _____   **71** slap + ed _____

| 8 |

Add one of the **prefixes** to each word to make its **antonym**.

un   in   im

72 _____ expensive   **73** _____ possible

74 _____ kind   **75** _____ practical

76 _____ perfect   **77** _____ done

| 6 |

Write whether each of these sentences is in the **past**, **present** or **future** tense.

78 I am eating. _____

79 I will swim. _____

80 I am reading. _____

81 I ran home. _____

82 I will brush my teeth. _____

83 I have done my homework. _____

| 6 |

Underline the **connectives** (word or words that join clauses or phrases) in each sentence.

84 The river broke its bank and many houses were flooded.

85 Dan cut himself, however, he didn't need a plaster.

86 Jane felt unwell, nevertheless she still went to school.

87 Harry agreed to go to the playground though he really wanted to go straight home.

88 Sam was given a prize but Henry has never won one.

89 The children weren't tired although it was past their bedtime.

6

Write the **antonym** for each of these words.

90 near _____   **91** over _____

92 top _____   **93** in _____

94 day _____   **95** hot _____

6

Circle the words which have a soft *g*.

96–100   gate   giraffe   vegetable   game

gem   page   magic   goblin   wagon

5

100
TOTAL

Paper 5

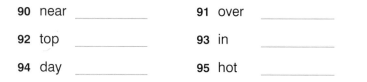

Camouflage

Many animals are camouflaged by being of similar colour to the places where they live. The polar bear who lives in the snowy far north has white fur. The kangaroo, who lives in dry, dusty grassland, has sandy-coloured fur. The colour of the lion blends in with the colour of dry grass found in hot countries. The tapirs, who live in the jungles, have a colour pattern which seems of little use – the front of their bodies, their heads and their legs are black, while the rest is white. We can pick out tapirs easily at the zoo but in their homeland it is not so. They hunt at night when there are patches of moonlight and patches of shadow and this is how they are protected. Some animals, like the Arctic fox, who live in cold countries change the colour of their coats in winter so that the new white coat will tone in with the snow. Other animals have a dazzle pattern. A zebra's black and white stripes don't blend in with its surroundings, but zebras feed in the early morning and late evening when they cannot be seen so well. Their outline is broken up against the tall grasses and trees and they become almost invisible.

Underline the correct answers.

1 What colour is a polar bear's fur?
(white, brown, sandy)

2 What environment does a kangaroo live in?
(jungle, snowy far north, dry dusty grassland)

3–4 Which two animals are black and white?
(polar bear, tapir, lion, Arctic fox, zebra)

4

Answer these questions.

5 Which animal lives in a hot country and has a coat the colour of dry grass?

_____

6–7 Which animal changes the colour of its coat in winter? Why?

_____

_____

8 Why are tapirs' coats the colour they are?

_____

9 Write a definition for the word 'camouflage'.

_____

10 Why don't farm animals and pets need to be camouflaged?

_____

6

Change each of these plurals into its **singular** form.

11 churches	_____	12 classes	_____
13 dresses	_____	14 bushes	_____
15 boxes	_____	16 dishes	_____
17 bunches	_____	18 foxes	_____

8

Underline the **pronouns** in the sentences.

19–20 Mine is smaller than yours.

21–22 I am glad they have bought a dog.

23–24 You need to buy him a present.

25–26 Have you taken mine?

27–28 We have put ours over there.

10

Rewrite these book titles, adding the missing capital letters.

29–31 jason saves the day

_____

32–34 the history of the vikings

_____

35–38 football skills made fun

_____

10

Write a **synonym** for each of the words in bold.

39 The sailors were told to **abandon** the ship.

40 The airman received an award for his **heroic** deed.

41 I have **sufficient** money to buy it.

42 She **enquired** how long she would have to wait.

43 The **entire** school went on the outing.

44 The children **dispersed** in all directions.

45 The athlete **encountered** many difficulties.

7

Add the missing apostrophes to each sentence.

46 Wheres your basket?

47 Isnt it over there?

48 Youll do it soon.

49 Dont do that!

50 I couldnt open the door.

51 We shouldve let her play with us.

52 Well have to go next time.

7

Put these towns in **alphabetical order**.

    Norwich   Northwich   Northampton

    Nottingham   Norwood   Northallerton

53 (1) _____   **54** (2) _____

55 (3) _____   **56** (4) _____

57 (5) _____   **58** (6) _____

    6

Write a second **clause** for each of these sentences.

59 The day was passing quickly because _____

_____

60 Naomi had a bath when _____

_____

61 The horse bolted as _____

_____

62 Tony worked hard at his tennis but _____

_____

63 The curtains were drawn in Ben's bedroom as _____

_____

64 The children quietly counted the money as _____

_____

65 Nan baked the cake secretly because _____

_____

    7

Add the **suffix** to each of these words.

66 safe + ly   _____   **67** hope + fully   _____

68 place + ment   _____   **69** nice + ly   _____

70 peace + ful   _____   **71** agree + ment   _____

    6

Circle the **preposition** (a word that relates other words to each other) in each of these sentences.

72 The river flowed down the valley.

73 Karen hid behind the sofa.

74 Pete and Emma struggled through the snow.

75 The zoo was behind the railway station.

76 Mum slept in the deckchair.

77 The cat jumped on the mouse.

78 The queen gracefully walked down the stairs.

79 The fish darted among the weeds.

REQUIRED IMMEDIATELY

A boy or girl to deliver newspapers

Hours – 6.30 a.m. to 8.00 a.m. Mondays to Saturdays

Wages £4 per day

It would be an advantage if the applicant had a bicycle

Write to:
Mr Jones
Newsagent
Pensby Rd
Moreton

Underline the statements that are correct.

80–85 The boy or girl must have a bicycle.

He/She would be needed six days a week.

Mr Jones wants a newsboy or girl quickly.

There is no hurry to reply.

The boy/girl would get paid £4 a week.

He/She would work nine hours a week.

The boy/girl must go to see Mr Jones.

Mr Jones doesn't mind if he employs a boy or a girl.

The pay would be £24 a week.

It would be a help if the girl/boy had a bicycle.

Write a word with the same letter string but a different pronunciation underlined in each of these words.

86 c<u>oo</u>k _____   87 ei<u>gh</u>t _____

88 thr<u>ough</u> _____   89 br<u>ave</u> _____

90 g<u>ive</u> _____   91 n<u>ow</u> _____   6

Add a powerful **verb** in the gaps to make each sentence interesting.

92 The children _____ over the bracken in their haste to get away.

93–94 Laila _____ at the top of her voice, making all the children

_____ .

95 The cow _____ towards the milking parlour.

96 Sam _____ while watching the horror movie.   5

Write four words that have entered our language in the last hundred years.

97–100 _____ _____ _____ _____   4

100 TOTAL

The Night Mail

This is the Night Mail crossing the Border,
Bringing the cheque and the postal order,

Letters for the rich, letters for the poor,
The shop at the corner, the girl next door.

Pulling up Beattock, a steady climb:
The gradient's against her, but she's on time.
Past cotton-grass and moorland boulder,
Shovelling white steam over her shoulder,

Snorting noisily, she passes
Silent miles of wind-bent grasses.

Birds turn their heads as she approaches,
Stare from bushes at her blank-faced coaches.

Sheep-dogs cannot turn her course;
They slumber on with paws across.

In the farm she passes no one wakes,
But a jug in a bedroom gently shakes.

Dawn freshens. Her climb is done.
Down towards Glasgow she descends,
Towards the steam tugs yelping down a glade of cranes,
Towards the fields of apparatus, the furnaces
Set on the dark plain like gigantic chessmen.
All Scotland waits for her:
In dark glens, beside pale-green lochs,
Men long for news.

by W H Auden

Underline the correct answers.

1 Beattock is a (town, hill, shop).

2 Birds turn their heads (to see what is making the noise, because they like watching trains, because they have stiff necks).

3 'Blank-faced coaches' are (ones with no lights, ones painted black, ones with no curtains).

Answer these questions.

4–6 What three items are we told the train is carrying?

_____

7 At what time of day does the train reach Glasgow?

_____

8 'Set on the dark plain like gigantic chessmen'. Write another word for 'gigantic'.

_____

9 Why do you think W H Auden describes the steam as 'over her shoulder'?

_____

10 Why do you think the people at the farm don't wake up as the train passes?

_____

Underline the **root word** of each of these words.

11 pressure 12 detective 13 blacken

14 recovered 15 signature 16 freshly

17 swimming 18 unhelpful

Circle the word which is . . .

19 a **pronoun** children came we go

20 a **verb** football goal play boys

21 an **adjective** dog friend him sad

22 an **adverb** speed I come quickly

23 a **noun** he aunt strong enrage

24 a **pronoun** there though it through

25 a **verb** teach children camera dinner

Underline the correct **homophone**.

26 The (lessen, lesson) started at eleven o'clock.

27 The man gave a (groan, grown) as he lifted his arms.

28 Dad said we must get a new ironing (board, bored).

29 The (lone, loan) sailor had crossed the ocean.

30 The gardener put in (steaks, stakes) for the sweet peas to climb.

31 Richard had (two, to) help his teacher.

32 Alice had an (hour, our) to wait.

7

Write a word which will describe each group of words, e.g. ant wasp bee fly *insects*

33 second   hour   minute   day   _____

34 doll   teddy-bear   ball   yo-yo   _____

35 London   Edinburgh   Paris   Madrid   _____

36 car   coach   bus   lorry   _____

37 chair   table   cupboard   desk   _____

38 tennis   football   cricket   hockey   _____

39 piano   drums   guitar   recorder   _____

7

With a line match each expression with its meaning.

40 hard up   to be treated badly

41 to get into hot water   to take punishment without complaint

42 to have forty winks   to get into trouble

43 to go on all fours   to ask for trouble

44 to play with fire   short of money

45 to face the music   to crawl on hands and knees

46 to lead a dog's life   to have a short sleep

7

Complete each sentence by adding a **conjunction**.

47 She didn't see me _____ I waved at her.

48 I have learned to swim _____ I have been at this school.

49 I cannot reach my books _____ you have moved that parcel.

50 David likes his tea very hot _____ Mary doesn't like tea at all.

51 I couldn't sing _____ I had a sore throat.

52 Kerry has cut her finger _____ she will have to wash it.

53 I am very keen on swimming _____ I like diving too.

7

Rewrite these words adding the **suffix** ery or ary. Make any spelling changes necessary.

54 burgle _____

55 brave _____

56 jewel _____

57 machine _____

58 slip _____

59 diction _____

60 discover _____

61 bound _____

8

Finish each sentence by adding a helper **verb** to match the **tense** in bold.

62 The car _____ speeding down the valley.   **past**

63 The birds _____ flying high in the sky.   **present**

64 A chicken _____ pecking in the dirt.   **present**

65 Two speed-boats _____ racing out to sea.   **past**

66 The sheep _____ flocking together on the moor.   **present**

67 A frog _____ jumping about in our pond.   **past**

6

Rewrite these sentences, adding the missing punctuation.

68–71 Can I have some of your drink asked Karen

_____

72–78 Are you up yet Jake's Mum called It is time for school

11

_____

Write the short form we often use for each of these words.

79 telephone _____

80 bicycle _____

81 examination _____

82 photograph _____

83 hippopotamus _____

84 mathematics _____

6

Barncroft Primary School, Portsmouth, is putting on a play, *Nelson's Adventures,* portraying the adventures of Nelson in his flagship, the *Victory*. The whole school has worked on this drama project for the last week after visiting the ship. Richard Edmunds, who plays Nelson, is reported to have said that it has been the best week at school he has ever had.

The children are performing to the general public on Friday 4th and Saturday 5th November at 7.30 p.m. Mrs Danielle Turnpike, the headteacher, would like to encourage people from the local area to come and watch as they might learn something new about the historic ship moored at their city. All the money the performances earn will be given to 'Children in Need'.

Answer these questions.

85 Barncroft Primary School is putting on a play. What is it about?

_____

86 Who is playing Nelson?

_____

87 On what days of the week are the performances?

_____

88 Why will the play be particularly interesting to the people of Portsmouth?

_____

4

Underline the **verb** in each of these sentences.

89 Climb the gate!

90 Get me a drink!

91 Run home quickly!

92 Jump on the box!

93 Grab me a towel!

94 Hang your coat over there!

6

Rewrite these sentences in the **future tense**.

95 I went skating.

_____

Some questions will be answered in the children's own words. Answers to these questions are given in *italics*. Any answers that seem to be in line with these should be marked correct.

Paper 1

1 palm tree
2 The inside
3 wetting them
4 *Around Madagascar.*
5 *Approximately 15 metres in length.*
6–7 *To dry and bleach them.*
8 *It is the fairest way as individual lengths would vary a great deal.*
9–10
   e.g. baskets, mats, containers, laundry baskets, lampshades
11–12
   scent, sent
13–14
   threw, through
15–16
   knot, not
17–18
   pane, pain
19–20
   stare, stairs
21 fire
22 first
23 flame
24 flap
25 flood
26 flop
27–29
   Sam loved going for walks, swimming in the duck pond, chasing rabbits, chewing a bone and sleeping in front of the fire.
30–31
   The baby cries when it is tired, hungry, has a tummy ache or has a dirty nappy.
32–34
   Jack wanted a new bike, some colouring pens, a computer game, new trainers and a pet dog for his birthday!
35–41
   gatepost, York, Monday, bunch, banana, violin, team
42 neatly
43 greedily
44 heavily
45 soundly
46 swiftly
47 suddenly
48 smartly
49 telephones
50 lanterns
51 museums

52 gorillas
53 chocolates
54 tissues
55 !
56 .
57 ! or .
58 ?
59 ?
60 .
61 !
62–64
   The girl ran to catch her bus.
65–66
   He/She had collected money to give to the homeless child.
67–69
   The lamb bounced towards its mother.
70–75
   We are going to Hull to see the docks.
   We will see several ships and if we are lucky they might let us look round them.
76 destroy
77 nasty
78 happy
79 kick
80 delighted
81 tiny
82 *Give yourself a hug*
83–84
   any two of: When you feel unloved, when people put on airs, when people give a cold-shoulder shrug.
85 *When people ignore you.*
86 *Yes.*
87 *It is saying that everyone is very special.*
88 careful
89 thoughtful
90 hopeful
91 shameful
92 wonderful
93 deceitful
94 the three dogs' collars
95 the two cars' horns
96 the five girls' jumpers
97 the two cinemas' screens
98 the three boys' books
99 the six birds' beaks
100 the two houses' chimneys

Paper 2

1 Monday
2 Thursday
3 Monday
4–5 elm, ash
6–7 Friday, Saturday
8–9 arm land
10 *[sentence stating favourite day of the week and why]*
11–17
   Seven of the following verbs: poured, flooded, bashed, came, walked, stood, was, bit, freeze, smashed, fell
18 **The goats pushed their way out of their pen** because they had spotted some apples.
19 **The cars raced past us** while we waited at the side of the motorway.
20 **Matthew's present was quickly hidden under the sofa** as he came in through the door.
21 **Some children wanted to go swimming** even though the water was freezing.
22 **The hat fitted perfectly** but it was the wrong colour.
23 **It started to rain heavily** as darkness fell over the sleepy village.
24 un**happy**
25 **jumped**
26 **quickly**
27 dis**placement**
28 un**certain**
29 af**fix**
30 un**tie**
31 **stronger**
32 mis**trusted**
33 cough
34 height
35 foot
36 have
37 both
38 move
39 flower
40 drought
41–42
   Yours looks longer than mine.
43–44
   Ours is smaller than his.
45–46
   Theirs runs faster than ours.
47 waiter

Answers

48 uncle
49 king
50 nephew
51 man
52 bull
53 father
54 brother
55 chief
56 field
57 weight
58 believe
59 eight
60 receive
61 vein
62 their
63–69
Prince Edward, Wednesday, London, Everton Football Club, Lucy Smith, River Severn, Parklands Primary School
70 Pass
71 Watch
72 Find
73 Run
74 Stop
75 Hurry
76–77
e.g. small, tiny
78–79
e.g. smooth, slippery
80–81
e.g. huge, massive
82 *Cross-Channel ferries*
83 *The Animal Magic Show*
84 *3.55*
85 *SMart*
86 *[answer stating choice of one programme listed and why they would choose it]*
87 *[answer stating programmes they think more relevant to children their age]*
88–95
[Eight different adverbs used in four sentences – e.g. quickly, silently, noisily, slowly, neatly, messily, quietly, hurriedly, thoughtfully, happily]
96 spaghetti
97 kangaroo
98 coffee or cocoa
99 tomato
100 *The last letter of each word is a vowel.*

Paper 3

1 It was larger than his
2 in two minutes
3 eighteen years

4–5 *Two of the following – built a wall around it, fixed guns to the wall, planted young trees around*
6 *His goats.*
7 *He would meet an enemy.*
8 *Next to the remains of a fire he found human bones.*
9–10 *[Two words describing how they would feel knowing cannibals were living on the same island as themselves – e.g. horrified, scared, terrified, frightened]*
11–21
My aunt, uncle and cousin came to stay with us last Wednesday. Next week we will catch a train to Birmingham. We are taking them to the theatre to see a pantomime called Aladdin. We will get back to our house very late.
22–25
"Come and hear the man play his banjo," called Tim.
26–29
"Where's my other slipper?" grumbled Grandpa.
30 *e.g. teacup, teaspoon*
31 *e.g. sunshine, sunglasses*
32 *e.g. snowball, snowflake*
33 *e.g. grandfather, grandmother*
34 *e.g. pillowcase*
35 *e.g. football, footfall*
36 *e.g. toothache, toothbrush*
37 *e.g. playtime, playground*
38 brushes
39 churches
40 punches
41 buses
42 thrushes
43 dresses
44–47
Hank shouted to Ben to hurry up.
Kay moaned that Debbie was always late.
The teacher told the children to leave by the fire exit.
Mum told Gran that David's school report was good.
48 driving
49 believing
50 making
51 caring
52 closing
53 wasting
54 waking
55 hoping
56 false
57 false
58 true
59 true
60 false

61 true
62 false
63 duck
64 sheep or goat
65 horse
66 dog
67 cat
68 snake
69 The wind swept over the barren landscape, tossing leaves high into the air.
70 Although the speeding train came off its rails, no one was hurt.
71 The lion crept up on its prey, ready to pounce.
72 Fed up because the computer continually broke down, they decided to buy a new one.
73 The sunbathers lay on the beach all afternoon, unaware of how burnt they were becoming.
74 Jess was delighted to see her mum, though she wished she had come to collect her earlier.
75–82
city, cereal, face, fleece, mice, lace, accident, ace
83 sound – found
84 high – sigh
85 fair – chair
86 bridge – fridge
87 follow – hollow
88 hatch – match
89 I fell over.
90 I feel hot.
91 I play football.
92 I walk home slowly.
93 I enjoy swimming.
94 I made some cakes.
95 *e.g. screamed*
96 *e.g. snatch*
97 *e.g. stroll*
98 *e.g. leap*
99 *e.g. create*
100 *e.g. collapse*

Paper 4

1 Victorian
2 to keep her warm
3 the dining room
4 Helen
5–6 *Two of the following instructions:*
weren't allowed to talk
had to walk everywhere quietly
always had to say 'Yes ma'am' or 'Yes sir'
7 *Baking bread in the kitchen.*

8 *The damp tea leaves would give the dust and dirt something to stick to.*

9 *[an answer stating which part of the trip they would have enjoyed the most and why]*

10 profound
11 bicycle
12 bilingual
13 provision
14 prolonged
15 biplane
16 proposition
17 pronoun
18 watch
19 plays
20 sweep
21 runs
22 win
23 swim
24 drops
25 root
26 night
27 adult
28 soldier
29 daisy
30 queue

31–32
[Two different sentences each ending with a question mark]

33–34
[Two different sentences each ending with a full-stop]

35–36
[Two different sentences each ending with an exclamation mark]

37–41
Flying squirrels glide.
Grey squirrels first came from America.
Squirrels are found in Europe and elsewhere.
Ground squirrels can dig a large number of burrows.
The most common squirrel in Europe is the red squirrel.

42 *e.g. colourful*
43 *e.g. huge*
44 *e.g. wooden*
45 *e.g. gold*
46 *e.g. smart*
47 *e.g. rickety*
48 *e.g. old*
49 *e.g. fluffy*
50 puppy
51 piglet
52 kitten
53 foal
54 calf
55 kid
56 duckling
57 chick

58 I'm never coming back./I'm not ever coming back.
59 Mark hasn't brought a towel for swimming.
60 The shopkeeper didn't have any fireworks.
61 There wasn't a teacher to help with my spelling./There was no teacher to help with my spelling.
62 Amy hasn't a coat to wear./Amy has no coat to wear.
63 There weren't any goats on the farm./There were no goats on the farm.
64 sitting
65 stopped
66 getting
67 walked
68 grinning
69 rotted
70 shopping
71 slapped
72 inexpensive
73 impossible
74 unkind
75 impractical
76 imperfect
77 undone
78 present
79 future
80 present
81 past
82 future
83 past
84 The river broke its bank <u>and</u> many houses were flooded.
85 Dan cut himself, <u>however</u>, he didn't need a plaster.
86 Jane felt unwell, <u>nevertheless</u> she still went to school.
87 Harry agreed to go to the playground <u>though</u> he really wanted to go straight home.
88 Sam was given a prize <u>but</u> Henry has never won one.
89 The children weren't tired <u>although</u> it was past their bedtime.
90 far
91 under
92 bottom
93 out
94 night
95 cold

96–100
giraffe, vegetable, gem, page, magic

Paper 5

1 white
2 dry dusty grassland
3–4 tapir, zebra
5 lion
6–7 *Arctic fox, to blend with the snow that arrives in winter.*
8 *Tapirs hunt at night and therefore that is when they need their camouflage.*
9 *a disguise*
10 *They don't need to hide from predators.*
11 church
12 class
13 dress
14 bush
15 box
16 dish
17 bunch
18 fox

19–20
<u>Mine</u> is smaller than <u>yours</u>.

21–22
<u>I</u> am glad <u>they</u> have bought a dog.

23–24
<u>You</u> need to buy <u>him</u> a present.

25–26
Have <u>you</u> taken <u>mine</u>?

27–28
<u>We</u> have put <u>ours</u> over there.

29–31
Jason **S**aves the **D**ay

32–34
The **H**istory of the **V**ikings

35–38
Football **S**kills **M**ade **F**un

39 *e.g. leave*
40 *e.g. brave*
41 *e.g. enough*
42 *e.g. asked*
43 *e.g. whole*
44 *e.g. scattered*
45 *e.g. met, faced*
46 Where's your basket?
47 Isn't it over there?
48 You'll do it soon.
49 Don't do that!
50 I couldn't open the door.
51 We should've let her play with us.
52 We'll have to go next time.
53 Northallerton
54 Northampton
55 Northwich
56 Norwich
57 Norwood
58 Nottingham

59–65
[completing the second clause for each of the sentences]

66 safely
67 hopefully
68 placement
69 nicely
70 peaceful
71 agreement
72 down
73 behind
74 through
75 behind
76 in
77 on
78 down
79 among
80–85
He/She would be needed six days a week.
Mr Jones wants a newsboy or girl quickly.
He/She would work nine hours a week.
Mr Jones doesn't mind if he employs a boy or a girl.
The pay would be £24 a week.
It would be a help if the girl/boy had a bicycle.
86 *[word with oo letter string but a pronunciation different from cook]*
87 *[word with igh letter string but a pronunciation different from eight]*
88 *[word with ough letter string but a pronunciation different from through]*
89 *[word with ave letter string but a pronunciation different from brave]*
90 *[word with ive letter string but a pronunciation different from give]*
91 *[word with ow letter string but a pronunciation different from now]*
92 *e.g. stumbled*
93–94
e.g. screamed, leap
95 *e.g. wandered*
96 *e.g. shuddered*
97–100 *e.g. grotty, hippy, television, grunge, rockumentary, docudrama, nerd, jukebox, reggae, website, dotcom, clone*

Paper 6

1 hill
2 to see what is making the noise
3 ones with no lights
4–6 *cheques, postal orders, letters*
7 *dawn*
8 *e.g. huge, big*

9 *As the train moves forward the steam is left leaving a trail over the shoulder of the train.*
10 *They would be used to the noise the train makes as it passes.*
11 pressure
12 detective
13 blacken
14 recovered
15 signature
16 freshly
17 swimming
18 unhelpful
19 we
20 play
21 sad
22 quickly
23 aunt
24 it
25 teach
26 lesson
27 groan
28 board
29 lone
30 stakes
31 to
32 hour
33 time
34 toys
35 cities
36 vehicles or transport
37 furniture
38 games or sport
39 instruments
40 hard up – short of money
41 to get into hot water – to get into trouble
42 to have forty winks – to have a short sleep
43 to go on all fours – to crawl on hands and knees
44 to play with fire – to ask for trouble
45 to face the music – to take punishment without complaint
46 to lead a dog's life – to be treated badly
47 *e.g. although*
48 *e.g. since*
49 *e.g. until*
50 *e.g. but*
51 *e.g. because*
52 *e.g. so*
53 *e.g. and*
54 burglary
55 bravery
56 jewellery
57 machinery
58 slippery
59 dictionary
60 discovery
61 boundary

62 was
63 are
64 is
65 were
66 are
67 was
68–71
"Can I have some of your drink?" asked Karen.
72–78
"Are you up yet?" Jake's Mum called. "It is time for school."
79 phone
80 cycle or bike
81 exam
82 photo
83 hippo
84 maths
85 *Nelson and his ship, the* Victory
86 *Richard Edmunds*
87 *Friday and Saturday*
88 *It will give them information about the historic ship moored at their city.*
89 Climb
90 Get
91 Run
92 Jump
93 Grab
94 Hang
95 I will/shall go skating.
96 She will take a photo.
97 I will/shall wake up at 7 o'clock.
98 I will/shall enjoy that piece of cake.
99 It will rain.
100 We will play on the swings.

Paper 7

1 It would give him food for three days.
2 rushed along shouting
3–4 *wild animals, the hyena*
5 *They would quickly finish the meat he had found.*
6 *No, he made it up to get rid of his children.*
7 *As animals heard the news they told friends and family and the message spread.*
8 *So many animals passed him on the way to the village that eventually the hyena thought that maybe he had been right and therefore headed to the village to find all the dead asses.*
9 basement
10 happiness
11 argument

12 spiteful
13 useful
14 soreness
15 Freda, the long-haired, cream-coloured cat, slept soundly.
16 The hollow-eyed, pale-faced mask frightened the children.
17 The huge, mottled brown horse bounded about the field.
18 Snow fell from the twisted, broken branch.
19 The cold and fresh water tasted lovely.
20 George put on his warm, cosy jumper.
21 The long, smooth snake hid under the rock for protection.
22 pizza – Italy
23 boomerang – Australia
24 wok – China
25 restaurant – France
26 moose – America
27 pyjamas – India
28 *e.g. quietly*
29 *e.g. angrily*
30 *e.g. loudly*
31 *e.g. well*
32 *e.g. softly*
33 *e.g. smugly*
34 *e.g. heartily*
35 *e.g. sternly*
36 Mark suddenly jumped, the dog having caught him unawares.
37–38
Time and time again, as the boat was tossed by the waves, the helicopter crew tried to save the fishermen.
39–40
The shop, which earlier had been bustling with shoppers, was now quiet.
41–42
Susie and Tariq, already soaked from the pouring rain, ran to find cover.
43–44 richer   richest
45–46 worse   worst
47–48 quieter   quietest
49–50 prettier   prettiest
51–52 more   most
53–54 earlier   earliest
55 fork
56 fortnight
57 web
58 elephant
59 puppet
60 nest
61 stage
62 string
63 halves
64 shelves

65 thieves
66 leaves
67 knives
68 calves
69–87
"Quick!" shouted Nina. "The water will trap us in the cave if we don't hurry."
"I know," screamed James trying to be heard above the thundering waves. As James ran, his feet barely touched the ground.
88 volcano
89 pizza
90 piano
91 umbrella
92 *The last letter of each word is a vowel.*
93 *ordinary* or *unattractive* or *simple*
94 *pull* or *drag* or *strain*
95 *force* or *persuade* or *poke* or *press*
96 pull
97–98
is, are
99 was
100 were

Paper 8

1–2 Missis, Pongo
3–5 were kind, did what they were told, were usually understanding
6 *four*
7 *They often guessed.*
8 *The humans believed they owned the dogs but it was the other way round.*
9 *Yes, he writes about them in a very warm and affectionate way.*
10–11
e.g. pretty   attractive
12–13
e.g. wrong   incorrect   left
14–15
e.g. happy   amused
16–17
e.g. mean   unkind
18–19
e.g. shout   yell
20 did
21 was
22 are
23 were
24 have
25 shall
26 has
27 will
28 traveller
29 rotten

30 knitted
31 foggy
32 running
33 fatter
34 sunny
35 flatten
36–40
The old lady walked slowly up the hill. She met a small boy who was singing happily as he cycled quickly to school. In the sweetshop the man spoke sternly to the tall girl who was leaning lazily against the counter.
41–44
Kelvin called,"It is time we went home."
45–48
"When can we go swimming?" asked Jenny.
49–52
"We will be late!" Mum yelled.
53 where
54 because
55 although
56 which
57 there
58 They're
59 their
60 there
61–62
their, their
63 They're
64–65
their, there
66 UK
67 CD
68 MP
69 USA
70 TV or telly
71 Dr
72 anything
73 nothing
74 anything
75 anything
76 nothing
77 nothing
78 Ben asked where his bag was.
79 Dad said we needed to be quick.
80 The children asked if they could go to the fair.
81 The teacher explained they were going to bake a cake.
82 *empty*
83 *hung*
84 *vain / proud*
85 *finished*
86 *cruelly*
87 *understood*
88 noun
89 noun
90 noun

91 verb
92 verb
93 verb
94 false
95 don't know
96 false
97 don't know
98 false
99 false
100 don't know

Paper 9

1 sunny
2–3 a farmer, me
4 *And gurgled awhile.*
5 *In the evening.*
6 *in the refreshment room*
7 *Home.*
8 *The last part of the journey home.*
9 *[an answer stating where the family could possibly have been, e.g. visiting family, on holiday]*
10 flies
11 bullies
12 babies
13 journeys
14 ladies
15 hobbies
16 cries
17 donkeys
18 drake
19 uncle
20 prince
21 nephew
22 landlord
23 king
24 up
25 with
26 from
27 over or up
28 behind
29 on or behind
30 Nan's knitting was finished at last.
31 Tony's dog ran away last week.
32 The two boys' football went over the fence.
33 The three rabbits' hutches fell down in the wind.
34 Caroline's leg hurt after she slipped on the ice.
35 My mother's bedroom was a mess.
36 *e.g. fight*
37 *e.g. dove*
38 *e.g. ridge*
39 *e.g. full*
40 *e.g. toast*

41 *e.g. more*
42 *e.g. strange*
43 *e.g. stitch*

44–52

	er	est	ish
long	longer	longest	longish
small	smaller	smallest	smallish
late	later	latest	latish

53 nowt – nothing
54 scoff – eat
55 wee – little
56 aye – yes
57 bairn – child
58 tatties – potatoes
59 skullache – headache

60–62
The candles blew out, plunging the children into darkness.

63–65
Carrying piles of apples, the carts were pulled down the road.

66–68
High in the sky, the birds were feeding on the flying insects.

69 UN
70 BBC
71 RAF
72 NATO
73 JP
74 WHO
75 CID

76–87
nouns: rabbit, cave, food, rock, remains, turnip, search;
adjectives: small, weak, mouldy;
verbs: searched, looking, could, find, were, sighed, continued;
adverbs: frantically, loudly;
prepositions: in, for, behind, of;
conjunctions: but, and

88–91
[four words with a soft c, e.g. city, circus, mice, face, dance]
92 He/She strokes the dog.
93 He/She cries loudly.
94 He/She washes his/her hair.
95 He/She cooks a meal.
96 *Night-time.*
97 *A rustling sound, like paper being trodden on.*
98 *The tooth-fairy.*
99 *whispering*
100 *It was Laith who made the rustling sound.*

Paper 10

1 night-time

2 as sharp as a knife
3 into her bed
4 *Black.*
5 *An arm was described as, 'thick as a tree-trunk'.*
6–9 *enormous long pale wrinkly*
10 *She was so scared she couldn't produce a sound.*
11 *[a sentence describing how they would have felt in the same situation as Sophie]*
12 *shyly*
13 *spied*
14 *tried*
15 *easier*
16 *drying*
17 *cried*

18–27
Suddenly, out of the tunnel emerged the **F**lying **S**cotsman. **H**annah and **L**eroy had been waiting for this moment, ever since reading about this train in **F**amous **T**rains of the **P**ast. They screamed with excitement as it flew past them on its way to **B**anbury.

28–29
e.g. everyone everything
30–31
e.g. candlelight candlestick
32–33
e.g. rainbow raindrop
34–35
e.g. playtime playground
36–40
[each of the listed adverbs written in a different sentence]

41–52

Common nouns	Proper nouns	Collective nouns	Abstract nouns
door	France	team	love
leg	Nigel	bunch	sympathy
camel	Hyde Park	swarm	justice

53 thief
54 elf
55 loaf
56 half
57 wolf
58 shelf
59–64
[adjectival phrases added in the gaps of sentences]
65 *e.g. detective*
66 *e.g. uncover*
67 *e.g. signature*
68 *e.g. attraction*
69 *e.g. statement*
70 *e.g. bicycle*
71 *e.g. meaning*
72 *e.g. helpful*
73 x

74 ✓
75 ✓
76 x
77 x
78 ✓
79 x

80–81
Dave ran with all his might when he saw the raging bull.

82–83
Julie combed her hair constantly because she wanted straight hair.

84–85
While Don was painting a picture, the lights suddenly went off.

86 ?
87 !
88 ?
89 !
90 ?
91 ?

92–94
e.g. whoosh, bang, zoom

95–97
e.g. plip plop, squelch, splash

98–100
e.g. moo, crunch, squeak

1 disappear quickly and quietly
2 people
3 brown
4 It enables them to hear people a mile away
5–6 Their feet grow natural leather soles and they are covered in thick warm brown hair.
7 They enjoy their food because eating makes them feel happy.
8 kind-looking face
9–11 [they need to describe how they see people's height, hands and eyes as if they were a hobbit]

12–20
dinner, diner, bath, bathe, sit, thorough, pasted, lung, lunge
21 sky
22 story
23 lorry
24 baby
25 berry
26 posy

27–28
[a sentence including the possessive pronouns, yours and ours]

29–30
[a sentence including the possessive pronouns, theirs and his]

31–32
[a sentence including the possessive pronouns, hers and mine]

33 e.g. because
34 e.g. but
35 e.g. but
36 e.g. until
37 e.g. when
38 e.g. and
39 e.g. but/although
40 telephone
41 automotive
42 circumnavigate
43 biplane
44 television
45 autobiography
46 telescope
47 bifocals

48–65
Nouns: coffee, horror, scoundrel
Verbs: thought, thrust, report
Adjectives: strange, whitish, sheer
Adverbs: early, really, almost
Prepositions: of, into, with
Pronouns: it, himself, you

66 was
67–68
were   was
69 was
70 were
71–72
were   was
73 was
74 head
75 blanket
76 leaf
77 music
78 horse
79 rat
80 fence
81 [a sentence including the preposition against, e.g. He leaned against the wall.]
82 [a sentence including the preposition between, e.g. She sat between Dave and me.]
83 [a sentence including the preposition through, e.g. The dog ran through the gate.]
84 [a sentence including the preposition behind, e.g. I hid behind the shed.]

85–92

France	Italy
café	pasta
boutique	umbrella

India	Turkey
chutney	doner-kebab
bungalow	yogurt

93 we'll
94 they'll
95 shouldn't
96 I've
97 hasn't
98 won't
99 there's
100 you're

1 India
2 people
3 six hundred years ago
4–6 He thought that the snake-god might bring fire, or plague or destroy the world
7–8 He told them to offer prayers and sacrifices to the snake-god
9 as hard as he could
10 e.g. pacify, calm, soothe
11 [a wish they would make as a Hindu king]
12 imperfect
13 incorrect
14 inaccurate
15 impure
16 imbalance
17 incomplete
18 immature
19 invisible
20 Mum called that it was time for dinner.
21 The children asked if they could go out to play.
22 David whispered to Amie that he was hiding in the shed.
23 The postman mumbled that it was really cold today.
24 Gina exclaimed that she loved her new shoes.
25 e.g. crackle
26 e.g. gasp, pant
27 e.g. squelch
28 e.g. thump
29 e.g. slam
30 e.g. splash
31 e.g. beep, beep
32 fitted
33 carried

Answers

34 knotted

35 picked

36 married

37 hunted

38 *e.g. Tom ate his food because he was very hungry.*

39 *e.g. The sun shone brightly and woke Gemma up.*

40 *e.g. The school trip was great fun and they didn't want to go home.*

41 *e.g. Nasar learnt his spelling homework but he still got some wrong in the test.*

42 past

43 past

44 present

45 present

46 future

47 past

48 future

49–60

noun beauty bread

adjective silky fluffy

verb stumbled heaved

adverb frantically stupidly

preposition of among

conjunction because although

61 *tried*

62 *asked*

63 *said*

64 *stuck*

65 *often*

66 *given*

67 *rich*

68 *clapped*

69 attract

70 entertain

71 depart

72 attach

73 fail

74 complete

75 *away*

76 *clock*

77 *makes*

78 *fill*

79 *drain*

80 *stair*

81 *same*

82 I haven't got any money.

83 There wasn't a clown at the circus.

84 There weren't any sweets in the jar./There were no sweets in the jar.

85 Tina hasn't an umbrella for the rain.

86–100

"Quick, come here!" called Tom. The rain was falling heavily and they wanted to avoid getting wet. "When do you think it will stop?" asked Misha.

96 She took a photo.

_____

97 I woke up at 7 o'clock.

_____

98 I enjoyed that piece of cake.

_____

99 It is raining.

_____

100 We played on the swings.

_____

Paper 7

The hyena once had the luck to come upon a dead ass. There was enough meat for three whole days. He was busy enjoying his meal when suddenly he saw his children coming. He knew their healthy young teeth and growing appetites, and as he did not want to share the magnificent carcass with them, he said: "You see that village over there? If you're quick you'll find plenty of asses there, just like this one. Only run."

The hyena's children rushed towards the village, shouting the news at the top of their voices. As the tale travelled to all corners of the bush, starving animals crept out – jackals, civet-cats, tiger-cats – all the smaller wild animals ran towards the village where the feast of asses' meat was to be found.

The whole morning the hyena watched them go by, singly or in flocks, until in the end he began to be worried.

Well, he said to himself, it looks as if it must be true. That village must be full of dead asses. And leaving the carcass he had had all to himself, he started off to join a band of other animals who were running towards the village.

The Hyena and the Dead Ass a West African tale retold by René Guillot

Underline the correct answers.

1 Why was the hyena lucky to find a dead ass?
(It would keep him warm at night, It would feed his family, It would give him food for three days)

2 What did the hyena's children do on their way to the village?
(crept along quietly, rushed along shouting, crept along shouting)

3–4 Who joined the hyena's children at the village?
(wild animals, only jackals, the hyena, only small wild animals)

4

Answer these questions.

5 Why didn't the hyena want his children to eat with him?

_____

6 Were there plenty of dead asses at the village?

_____

7 How do you think the tale of the dead asses travelled to the corners of the bush?

_____

8 Why do you think the hyena joined the other animals in running towards the village?

_____

Add the **suffix** to each of these words. Don't forget spelling changes.

9 base + ment _____

10 happy + ness _____

11 argue + ment _____

12 spite + ful _____

13 use + ful _____

14 sore + ness _____

Underline the **adjectival phrase** in each sentence.

15 Freda, the long-haired, cream-coloured cat, slept soundly.

16 The hollow-eyed, pale-faced mask frightened the children.

17 The huge, mottled brown horse bounded about the field.

18 Snow fell from the twisted, broken branch.

19 The cold and fresh water tasted lovely.

20 George put on his warm, cosy jumper.

21 The long, smooth snake hid under the rock for protection.

With a line match the country from where you think each word is borrowed.

22 pizza   Australia

23 boomerang   China

24 wok   Italy

25 restaurant   America

26 moose   India

27 pyjamas   France

Complete each sentence using an **adverb**.

28 I whispered _____ .

29 We shouted _____ .

30 I coughed _____ .

31 We slept _____ .

32 I cried _____ .

33 We chuckled _____ .

34 I laughed _____ .

35 We argued _____ .

8

Add the missing commas to these sentences.

36 Mark suddenly jumped the dog having caught him unawares.

37–38 Time and time again as the boat was tossed by the waves the helicopter crew tried to save the fishermen.

39–40 The shop which earlier had been bustling with shoppers was now quiet.

41–42 Susie and Tariq already soaked from the pouring rain ran to find cover.

7

Complete the following **adjectives** of comparison.

      e.g.   good   _better_   _best_

43–44 rich _____ _____

45–46 bad _____ _____

47–48 quiet _____ _____

49–50 pretty _____ _____

51–52 many _____ _____

53–54 early _____ _____

12

Give one word for each of these **definitions**.

55 Can be used when eating. It has three or four prongs set on the end of a handle. _____

56 A period of two weeks. _____

57 A network of fine threads spun by a spider to catch insects. _____

58 A big, four-legged animal with tusks and a long trunk. _____

59 A doll worked by pulling wires or strings in a toy theatre. _____

60 Made by birds as a place in which to lay eggs and bring up their young. _____

61 A raised platform on which plays are often performed. _____

62 Thin rope, line or cord used for tying up parcels. _____   8

Write each of these words in their **plural** form.

63 half _____   **64** shelf _____

65 thief _____   **66** leaf _____

67 knife _____   **68** calf _____   6

Copy the passage, adding the missing capital letters and punctuation.

69–87 quick shouted nina the water will trap us in the cave if we don't hurry
I know screamed james trying to be heard above the thundering waves
as james ran his feet barely touched the ground

_____

_____

_____

_____   19

_____

Write a word to match each picture.

88   **89**

_____   _____

90   **91**

_____   _____   4

37

92 What do you notice about the last letter of each of the words (Questions **88–91**)?

pick	choice, choose, gather
piece	bit, chip, part, splinter, slice
pile	heap, collection, stack
plain	ordinary, unattractive, simple
pull	drag, tow, strain
push	force, persuade, poke, press

93 Write a word that has a similar meaning to 'plain'.

94 Write a word that has a similar meaning to 'tow'.

95 Write a synonym for the word 'push'.

96 Next to which word in bold would you put
the word 'tug'?

Underline the correct word in brackets.

97–98 An ambulance (is, are) speeding to the accident as many people (is, are) hurt.

99 There (was, were) a party at Sonia's house.

100 Many children (was, were) enjoying the firework display.

Paper 8

Not long ago, there lived in London a young married couple of Dalmatian dogs named Pongo and Missis Pongo. (Missis had added Pongo's name to her own on their marriage, but was still called Missis by most people.) They were lucky enough to own a young married couple of humans named Mr. and Mrs. Dearly, who were gentle, obedient, and usually intelligent – almost canine at times. They understood quite a number of barks: the bark for "Out, please!" "In, please!" "Hurry up with my dinner!" and "What about a walk?" And even when they could not understand, they could often guess – if looked at soulfully or scratched by an eager paw. Like many other much-loved humans, they believed that they owned their dogs, instead of realising that their dogs owned them. Pongo and Missis found this touching and amusing and let their pets think it was true.

From *101 Dalmatians* by Dodie Smith

Underline the correct answers.

1–2　The dogs' names were (Missis, Dearly, Pongo, Dalmatian).

3–5　Their owners (were kind, were old, were slow, did what they were told, were unintelligent, were usually understanding).

5

Answer these questions.

6　How many barks did the Dearlys understand?

_____

7　What did the Dearlys do if they didn't understand what the dogs were barking?

_____

8　Why were the dogs 'touched and amused'?

_____

9　Do you think Dodie Smith, the author of *101 Dalmatians,* likes dogs? Why?

4

_____

Write two **antonyms** for each word.

10–11 ugly _____ _____

12–13 right _____ _____

14–15 sad _____ _____

16–17 kind _____ _____

18–19 whisper _____ _____

10

Underline the correct word in the brackets.

20 Tim (done, did) his homework.

21 Every boy (were, was) on the field.

22 They (are, was) late today.

23 All the men (were, was) working.

24 I (have, shall) eaten all the cakes.

25 We (have, shall) take the dog for a walk.

26 I dropped the bag but not one of the eggs (has, shall) broken.

27 They (will, were) collect the old bed.

8

Add the **suffix** to each word. Make any necessary spelling changes.

28 travel + er _____   **29** rot + en _____

30 knit + ed _____   **31** fog + y _____

32 run + ing _____   **33** fat + er _____

34 sun + y _____   **35** flat + en _____

8

Underline the **adverbs** in the following passage.

36–40 The old lady walked slowly up the hill. She met a small boy who was singing happily as he cycled quickly to school. In the sweetshop the man spoke sternly to the tall girl who was leaning lazily against the counter.

5

Rewrite these sentences and add the missing punctuation.

41–44 Kelvin called It is time we went home

_____

45–48 When can we go swimming asked Jenny

_____

49–52 We will be late Mum yelled

_____

In each gap add a **connective**.

although   where   because   which

53 The ship had called at many ports, finally arriving in Dublin _____ the sailors could go on leave.

54 Wendy was soaking _____ she had fallen in the river.

55 Daniel always found maths very difficult _____ he tried very hard.

56 Mum bought a new jumper _____ came with a free skirt.

Write _there, their_ or _they're_ in each of the gaps. Don't forget capital letters, if necessary.

57 I would like to go _____ today.

58 _____ waiting for the bus.

59 I like the colour of _____ school uniform.

60 "What a huge amount of work _____ is to do," sighed Mark.

61–62 The children were told to put _____ books inside _____ bags.

63 _____ very quiet!

64–65 They put _____ coats over _____ .

Write the **abbreviations** (shortened form) of these words.

66 United Kingdom   _____

67 compact disc   _____

68 Member of Parliament   _____

69 United States of America   _____

70 television   _____

71 Doctor   _____

Add *anything* or *nothing* to each of these sentences.

72 David didn't say _____ as he travelled to school.

73 "There is _____ to do," moaned Tanya.

74 Nasar can't find _____ in his messy room.

75 Sonia didn't have _____ for breakfast.

76 There is _____ to paint with.

77 It is _____ to do with me!

6

Rewrite these sentences as **reported speech**.

78 "Where is my bag?" asked Ben.

_____

79 "We need to be quick," said Dad.

_____

80 "Can we go to the fair?" asked the children.

_____

81 "We are going to bake a cake," the teacher explained.

_____

4

Write a **synonym** for the word in bold.

82 The house was **vacant** for some time. _____

83 It was **suspended** from the ceiling. _____

84 The girl was very **conceited**. _____

85 Michael had **completed** his work. _____

86 He treated the horse **brutally**. _____

87 She **comprehended** what the man said. _____

6

Write whether each word is a **noun** or a **verb**.

e.g. inform   *verb*

88 suggestion _____

89 cloudiness _____

42

90 conservation _____

91 discuss _____

92 insulate _____

93 specialise _____

NO DOGS IN OUR PLAYGROUND

Keep dogs away from our playground because . . .

❏ they frighten some children

❏ they get in the way of the swings

❏ they leave a mess

Please walk your dogs in the park area around the duck pond.

Write *true*, *false* or *don't know* next to each statement.

94 Dogs are allowed in the playground. _____

95 There is a slide in the playground. _____

96 Dogs frighten all children. _____

97 Dogs should be walked in the park area. _____

98 Dogs can be in the playground if they are with their owners. _____

99 Dogs never leave a mess. _____

100 The park has a duck pond. _____

Paper 9

Journey Home

I remember the long homeward ride, begun
By the light that slanted in from the level sun;
And on the far embankment, in sunny heat,
Our whole train's shadow travelling dark and complete.
A farmer snored. Two loud gentlemen spoke
Of the cricket and news. The pink baby awoke
And gurgled awhile. Till slowly out of the day
The last light sank in glimmer and ash-grey.
I remember it all; and dimly remember, too,
The place where we changed – the dark trains lumbering through;
The refreshment room, the crumbs, and the slopped tea;
And the salt on my face, not of tears, not tears, but the sea.
"Our train at last!" said Father. "Now tumble in!
It's the last lap home!" And I wondered what 'lap' could mean;
But the rest is all lost, for a huge drowsiness crept
Like a yawn upon me; I leant against Mother and slept.

by John Walsh

Underline the correct answers.

1 The weather was (cold, stormy, sunny, grey).

2–3 In the poem two people slept. Who were they?
(a gentleman, a farmer, me).

3

Answer these questions.

4 What words show that the baby might be happy?

_____

5 At what time of the day were the family travelling?

_____

6 Where did the family wait for their second train?

_____

7 Where were the family travelling to?

_____

8 What do you think 'the last lap home' means?

_____

9 Where do you think the family had been?

_____ `6`

Write each of these words in its **plural form**.

10 fly _____ **11** bully _____

12 baby _____ **13** journey _____

14 lady _____ **15** hobby _____

16 cry _____ **17** donkey _____ `8`

Write the masculine form of each of these words.

18 duck _____ **19** aunt _____

20 princess _____ **21** niece _____

22 landlady _____ **23** queen _____ `6`

Write a suitable **preposition** in each gap.

on   with   behind   over   from   up

24 He ran _____ the stairs.

25 The teacher was cross _____ the cheeky boy.

26 Your T-shirt is different _____ mine.

27 The boy climbed _____ the wall.

28 The mouse hid _____ the bush.

29 Dad hid the present _____ the cupboard. `6`

Rewrite these sentences, adding the missing apostrophes.

30 Nans knitting was finished at last.

_____

31 Tonys dog ran away last week.

_____

32 The two boys football went over the fence.

_____

33 The three rabbits hutches fell down in the wind.

_____

34 Carolines leg hurt after she slipped on the ice.

_____

35 My mothers bedroom was a mess.

_____

6

Next to each word write another word with the same spelling pattern.

36 light _____ **37** love _____

38 bridge _____ **39** bull _____

40 boast _____ **41** core _____

42 range _____ **43** ditch _____

8

Complete the table below.

44–52

	er	est	ish
long			
small			
late			

9

With a line match the **dialect** words with their meaning.

53 nowt   eat

54 scoff   potatoes

55 wee   child

56 aye   yes

57 bairn   headache

58 tatties   nothing

59 skullache   little

7

Copy these sentences and add the missing punctuation and capital letters.

60–62 the candles blew out plunging the children into darkness

_____

63–65 carrying piles of apples the carts were pulled down the road

_____

66–68 high in the sky the birds were feeding on the flying insects

_____

9

Abbreviate these words into their **abbreviations** or **acronyms**.

69 United Nations   _____

70 British Broadcasting Corporation   _____

71 Royal Air Force   _____

72 North Atlantic Treaty Organisation   _____

73 Justice of the Peace   _____

74 World Health Organisation   _____

75 Criminal Investigation Department   _____

7

Use words from the passage to complete the table.

> The small, weak rabbit searched frantically in the cave looking for food but all it could find behind a rock were the remains of a mouldy turnip. The rabbit sighed loudly and continued the search.

76–87

noun	adjective	verb	adverb	preposition	conjunction

12

Write four words with a soft *c*.

88 _____   **89** _____

90 _____   **91** _____

4

Rewrite each sentence as though you are writing about someone else.

e.g. I feel cold.   *She feels cold.*

92 I stroke the dog.   _____

93 I cry loudly.   _____

94 I wash my hair.   _____

95 I cook a meal.   _____

4

It is night-time and Laith and Karen are in bed pretending to be asleep – they are waiting for the tooth-fairy; a quiet rustling noise is heard.

(whispering)

Laith   Karen are you awake?

Karen   I might be!

Laith   Did you hear that?

Karen   No . . . what?

Laith   That sound, like paper being trodden on.

Karen   You are imagining things. There isn't such a thing as a tooth-fairy. I'm tired . . . I'm going to sleep now.

Silence for a few moments then the rustling sound again. Karen sits bolt upright in her bed.

Karen   Laith . . . I heard it that time!

Laith giggles.

Answer these questions.

96 What time of day is it?

_____

97 What sound did they hear?

_____

98 What are Laith and Karen waiting for?

_____

99 What word describes how the children are talking to each other?

_____

100 Why do you think Laith giggles?

_____

5

100
TOTAL

Paper 10

In the moonlight, Sophie caught a glimpse of an enormous long pale wrinkly face with the most enormous ears. The nose was as sharp as a knife, and above the nose there were two bright flashing eyes, and the eyes were staring straight at Sophie. There was a fierce and devilish look about them.

Sophie gave a yelp and pulled back from the window. She flew across the dormitory and jumped into her bed and hid under the blanket.

And there she crouched, still as a mouse, and tingling all over.

Under the blanket Sophie waited.

After a minute or so, she lifted a corner of the blanket and peeped out.

For the second time that night her blood froze to ice and she wanted to scream, but no sound came out. There at the window, with the curtains pushed aside, was the enormous long pale wrinkly face of the Giant Person, staring in. The flashing black eyes were fixed on Sophie's bed.

The next moment, a huge hand with pale fingers came snaking in through the window. This was followed by an arm, an arm as thick as a tree-trunk, and the arm, the hand, the fingers were reaching out across the room towards Sophie's bed.

From *The BFG* by Roald Dahl

Underline the correct answers.

1 At what time of day does the passage take place?
(day-time, night-time, can't tell)

2 How was the Giant Person's nose described?
(as long as a knife, as pointed as a knife, as sharp as a knife)

3 Where did Sophie run to?
(the other side of the room, into her bed, behind the curtain)

3

Answer these questions.

4 What was the colour of the Giant Person's eyes?

_____

5 What words in the passage tell us the Giant Person had very thick arms?

_____

6–9 Write four adjectives that describe the Giant Person's face.

_____ _____ _____ _____

10 Why do you think that when Sophie wanted to scream no sound came out?

_____

11 Write a sentence describing how you would have felt if you were Sophie and the Giant Person's fingers were reaching across to you.

_____

_____

8

Add the **suffix** to each of these words. Don't forget any spelling changes.

12 shy + ly _____

13 spy + ed _____

14 try + ed _____

15 easy + er _____

16 dry + ing _____

17 cry + ed _____

6

Copy the passage, adding the missing capital letters.

18–27 suddenly, out of the tunnel emerged the flying scotsman. hannah and leroy had been waiting for this moment, ever since reading about this train in famous trains of the past. they screamed with excitement as it flew past them on its way to banbury.

_____

_____

_____

_____

_____

| 10 |

Write two **compound words** that begin with the word in bold.

28–29 every _____   _____

30–31 candle _____   _____

32–33 rain _____   _____

34–35 play _____   _____

| 8 |

Write each of these **adverbs** in a sentence.

36 angrily

_____

37 quickly

_____

38 cleverly

_____

39 stupidly

_____

40 unexpectedly

_____

| 5 |

Complete the table of **nouns** below.

41–52   France   love   team   door   sympathy   leg   Nigel

camel   justice   bunch   swarm

Hyde Park

Common nouns	Proper nouns	Collective nouns	Abstract nouns

12

Write each of these words in their **singular** form.

53 thieves _____   **54** elves _____

55 loaves _____   **56** halves _____

57 wolves _____   **58** shelves _____

6

Add an **adjectival phrase** to complete each sentence.

59 Yousef climbed the _____ stairs.

60 The goat, _____, staggered down the cliff.

61 Judith slept peacefully in her _____ bed.

62 The _____ fireworks went high in the sky.

63 Alice clutched her _____ teddy.

64 Monty, the _____ dog, bounded through the long grass.

6

Add a **suffix** and/or **prefix** to each of these **root words** to make a new word.

65 detect _____   **66** cover _____

67 sign _____   **68** attract _____

69 state _____   **70** cycle _____

71 mean _____   **72** help _____

8

Put a *tick* next to the words spelt correctly and a *cross* next to those spelt incorrectly.

73 shreik ___

74 rein ___

75 leisure ___

76 releive ___

77 neice ___

78 receive ___

79 seige ___

7

Underline the two **clauses** in each sentence.

80–81 Dave ran with all his might when he saw the raging bull.

82–83 Julie combed her hair constantly because she wanted straight hair.

84–85 While Don was painting a picture, the lights suddenly went off.

6

Add the missing question marks or exclamation marks.

86 Are you happy ___

87 Keep smiling ___

88 Where are you going ___

89 Hurry up, we might be late ___

90 What is for tea ___

91 Do you like my hair ___

6

Write down three **onomatopoeic** words that can describe these.

92–94 fireworks

_____ _____ _____

95–97 rain

_____ _____ _____

98–100 a farmyard

_____ _____ _____

9

100
TOTAL

Paper 11

What is a hobbit? I suppose hobbits need some description nowadays since they have become rare and shy to the Big People, as they call us. They are (or were) a little people, about half our height, and smaller than the bearded Dwarves. Hobbits have no beards. There is little or no magic about them, except the ordinary everyday sort which helps them to disappear quietly and quickly when large stupid folk like you and me come blundering along, making a noise like elephants which they can hear a mile off. They are inclined to be fat in the stomach; they dress in bright colours (chiefly green and yellow); wear no shoes because their feet grow natural leather soles and thick warm brown hair like the stuff on their heads (which is curly); have long brown fingers, good natured faces and laugh deep fruity laughs (especially after dinner which they have twice a day when they can get it).

From *The Hobbit* by J R R Tolkien

Underline the correct answers.

1 What magic can hobbits do?
   (make themselves smaller, disappear quickly and quietly, make magic shoes)

2 What creatures do hobbits think make a lot of noise?
   (elephants, dwarves, people)

3 What colour is a hobbit's skin?
   (white, black, pink, brown)

3

Answer these questions.

4 Why might good hearing be an advantage to hobbits?

_____

5–6 Write two reasons why hobbits don't need to wear shoes.

_____

7 Explain why you think hobbits enjoy their food.

_____

8 Hobbits have 'good natured faces'. Describe what this means.

_____

9–11 Imagine you are a hobbit. Describe these three things about hobbits.

height _____

hands _____

eyes _____

Circle the words that *aren't* **homophones**.

12–20   diner   dinner   vain   vein   vane   bath   bathe

cite   site   sight   sit   through   thorough   threw

rain   reign   rein   passed   past   pasted

grisly   grizzly   lung   lunge   missed   mist

Change these words into their **singular** form.

21 skies _____   **22** stories _____

23 lorries _____   **24** babies _____

25 berries _____   **26** posies _____

Write a sentence for each pair of **possessive pronouns**.

27–28 yours, ours

_____

29–30 theirs, his

_____

31–32 hers, mine

_____

Add a **conjunction** to complete each sentence.

33 Robert couldn't run _____ he had hurt his foot.

34 The rain poured in through the window _____ no one noticed.

35 I knew where my toothbrush should be _____ I couldn't find it.

36 The dog scratched at the door _____ someone let him in.

37 I like fish and chips _____ I am feeling hungry.

38 Sheena loves reading _____ also writing stories.

39 Deano was tired _____ he didn't want to go to bed.

Choose the correct **prefix** to complete each word.

bi   circum   auto   tele

40 _____ phone   **41** _____ motive

42 _____ navigate   **43** _____ plane

44 _____ vision   **45** _____ biography

46 _____ scope   **47** _____ focals

8

A very **strange** thing happened in Petersburg. The barber, Ivan, woke up **early** and detected the smell of freshly baked bread.

"Praskovia," he called to his wife, "I won't have **coffee** today. I'll just have a hot roll instead."

Ivan would **really** have liked both but he knew his wife would never put up with such whims. "Let the nitwit have bread," **thought** his wife to herself, "so I can have an extra cup **of** coffee." And she tossed a roll onto the table.

Ivan sat down at the table, took a knife, and proceeded to cut the roll in half. He peered **into** the middle of it, and to his surprise he noticed something **whitish** there. He poked it **with** his knife, and prodded **it** with his finger. "Something compact," he muttered to **himself**. "What can it be?"

He **thrust** in two fingers and pulled out – a nose! Ivan **almost** went to pieces; he rubbed his eyes and felt the thing again: a nose, it was undoubtedly a nose! And what's more, it looked somehow familiar. His face was a picture of **sheer** horror. But this **horror** was as nothing beside the rage which seized his wife.

"Where did you lop off that nose, **you** beast?" she shrieked. "You **scoundrel**! I'll **report** you to the police myself."

From 'The Nose', in *Petersburg Tales* by Nikolai Gogol, translated from the Russian by Diana Roberts

Put the words in bold in the correct spaces.

48–65 Nouns	Verbs	Adjectives
_____	_____	_____
_____	_____	_____
_____	_____	_____

Adverbs	**Prepositions**	**Pronouns**
_____	_____	_____
_____	_____	_____
_____	_____	_____

Add *was* or *were* in each gap to complete each sentence.

66 I _____ tired and hungry.

67–68 They _____ ready to go swimming but the pool _____ not open.

69 The kitten _____ playful.

70 All the children had finished their lunch and _____ ready to go out to play.

71–72 They _____ queuing for hours as the film _____ supposed to be brilliant.

73 Sam wondered whether it _____ time to get up.

8

Choose a word to complete each expression.

blanket   fence   head   rat   music   leaf   horse

74 to hang your _____

75 to be a wet _____

76 to turn over a new _____

77 to face the _____

78 to put the cart before the _____

79 to smell a _____

80 to sit on the _____

7

Use each of these **prepositions** in a sentence of your own.

81 against

_____

82 between

_____

83 through

_____

84 behind

_____

4

Complete the table below, matching each word with its country of origin.

85–92

café   chutney   pasta   doner-kebab

yogurt   boutique   bungalow   umbrella

France	Italy	India	Turkey

8

Write a **contraction** for each of these pairs of words.

93 we shall _____

94 they will _____

95 should not _____

96 I have _____

97 has not _____

98 will not _____

99 there is _____

100 you are _____

8

100 TOTAL

Paper 12

...ere is an old legend about Delhi (the capital of India). Long ago an old Hindu king was hammering a large iron nail into the earth, and as he swung with all his might the tip of the nail struck the head of the snake-god who supports the world on his coiled body. The king trembled at the thought of the snake-god's anger – would he bring fire and plague to his subjects, or even destroy the world? He ordered all his subjects to offer prayers and sacrifices to placate the snake-god. Several months passed and when the god's anger was soothed he told the king that he wouldn't punish him, but he said that on that spot there would always be war and unrest.

The iron nail in this fable is supposed to be the Iron Pillar which today stands in the courtyard of a tower built about six hundred years ago. There is another legend which says that if you stand with your back to the pillar and can stretch your arms behind you around the pillar, all your wishes will come true. Many people have tried to do this but no one has had arms long enough to get more than half way round the pillar!

Underline the correct answers.

1 In which country is the city of Delhi?
(India, Iran, Indonesia)

2 What are the king's 'subjects'?
(words, people, thoughts, towns)

3 How long ago was the tower that houses the Iron Pillar built?
(sixty years ago, six thousand years ago, six hundred years ago)

`3`

Answer these questions.

4–6 What three things was the king frightened the god might do?

_____

_____

_____

7–8 What two things did the king tell his people to do?

_____

_____

9 What does 'with all his might' mean?

_____

10 Write another word for 'placate'.

_____

11 If you were the Hindu king and one day all your wishes were granted, what would you wish for?

_____

_____

`8`

refix *in* or *im* to each of these words.

_____perfect   13 _____correct   14 _____accurate

15 _____pure   16 _____balance   17 _____complete

18 _____mature   19 _____visible

`8`

59

Rewrite these direct speech sentences into **reported speech**.

20 "Time for dinner," called Mum.

_____

21 "Can we go out to play?" asked the children.

_____

22 "I'm hiding in the shed," David whispered to Amie.

_____

23 "It is really cold today," mumbled the postman.

_____

24 "I love my new shoes," exclaimed Gina.

_____

5

Write an **onomatopoeic** word for each of the following.

25 a bag of crisps   _____

26 out of breath   _____

27 tramping through mud   _____

28 a bouncing ball   _____

29 closing a door   _____

30 diving in water   _____

31 a watch alarm   _____

7

Add the **suffix** _ed_ to each of these words. Don't forget any spelling changes.

32 fit   _____   **33** carry   _____

34 knot   _____   **35** pick   _____

36 marry   _____   **37** hunt   _____

Write each of these pairs of short sentences as one sentence.

38 Tom ate his food. He was very hungry.

_____

39 The sun shone brightly. It woke Gemma up.

_____

40 The school trip was great fun. They didn't want to go home.

_____

41 Nasar learnt his spelling homework. He still got some wrong in the test.

_____

4

Write whether each of these sentences is in the **past**, **present** or **future tense**.

42 The dog licked Grant. _____

43 Sandra was swimming. _____

44 Len is sleeping. _____

45 The chicken is laying an egg. _____

46 I shall not be home till six o'clock. _____

47 Cleo ate her food. _____

48 Rachel will come to Matthew's house. _____

7

Write the words in the correct columns of the table.

49–60

stumbled   frantically   because   of   silky   among

heaved   beauty   stupidly   fluffy   bread   although

noun	adjective	verb	adverb	preposition	conjunction

12

Write a **synonym** for each word in bold.

61 I **attempted** to climb the rock. _____

62 She was **requested** to sit down and wait. _____

63 He **remarked** that he was cold and tired. _____

64 The picture **adhered** to the paper. _____

65 She **frequently** went to see her grandmother. _____

66 Jack was **awarded** the first prize. _____

67 Shaun's family was very **wealthy**. _____

68 At the concert we **applauded** loudly. _____

8

Remove the **suffix** of these **abstract nouns** to make a **verb**.

69 attraction _____

70 entertainment _____

71 departure _____

72 attachment _____

73 failure _____

74 completion _____

6

Fill in the missing words in this poem.

> A stranger called this morning
> Dressed all in black and grey
> Put every sound into a bag

75 And carried them _____

> The whistling of the kettle
> The turning of the lock
> The purring of the kitten

76 The ticking of the _____

> The popping of the toaster
> The crunching of the flakes
> When you spread the marmalade

77 The scraping noise it _____

> The hissing of the frying-pan
> The ticking of the grill
> The bubbling of the bathtub

78 As it starts to _____

> The drumming of the raindrops
> On the window-pane
> When you do the washing-up

79 The gurgle of the _____

> The crying of the baby
> The squeaking of the chair
> The swishing of the curtain

80 The creaking of the _____

A stranger called this morning
He didn't leave his name
Left us only silence
81 Life will never be the _____

7

Rewrite these sentences without double negatives.

82 I haven't got no money.

_____

83 There wasn't no clown at the circus.

_____

84 There weren't no sweets in the jar.

_____

85 Tina hasn't no umbrella for the rain.

_____

4

Rewrite the following correctly.

86–100

quick come here called tom
the rain was falling heavily and they wanted to avoid getting wet
when do you think it will stop asked misha

_____

_____

_____

15

100
TOTAL

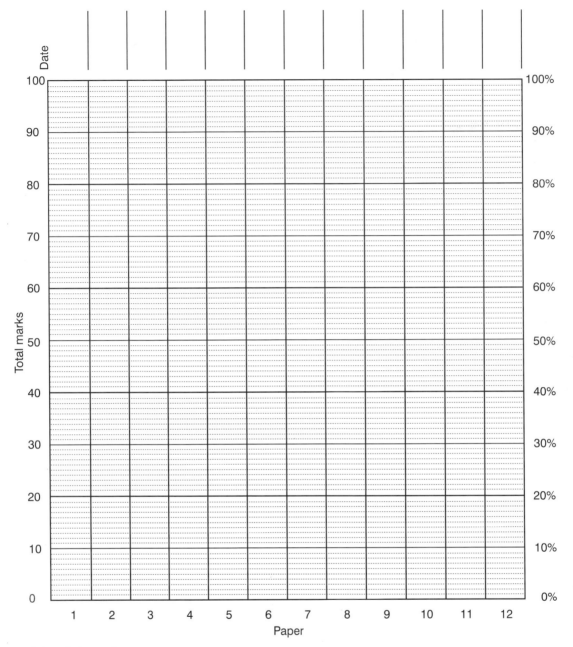

Date

Total marks

100 — 100%

90 — 90%

80 — 80%

70 — 70%

60 — 60%

50 — 50%

40 — 40%

30 — 30%

20 — 20%

10 — 10%

0 — 0%

1 2 3 4 5 6 7 8 9 10 11 12

Paper

Acknowledgements
The authors and publishers wish to thank the following for permission to use copyright material: 'Give Yourself a Hug', reproduced with permission of Curtis Brown Ltd, London, on behalf of Grace Nichols, copyright Grace Nichols 1994; 'A Week of Winter Weather' by Wes Magee; extract from 'Night Mail' by W H Auden, reproduced by permission of Faber & Faber Limited; *The Hyena and the Dead Ass* retold by René Guillot from *The Oxford Book of Animal Stories*, ed. Dennis Pepper 1994, reproduced by permission of Oxford University Press; extract from *101 Dalmatians* by Dodie Smith, reproduced by permission of the Literary Executor of the Estate of the late Dodie Smith; extract from *The BFG* by Roald Dahl, reproduced by permission of Jonathan Cape & Penguin Books; extract from *The Hobbit* by J R R Tolkien, reproduced by permission of Harper Collins Publishers Ltd; 'The Sound Collector' reprinted by permission of PFD on behalf of Roger McGough, © Roger McGough as printed in the original volume.

Every effort has been made to trace all copyright holders, but if any have been inadvertently overlooked the publishers will be pleased to make the necessary arrangements at the first opportunity.